TOOLS OF WAR

WEAPONS
and VEHICLES

of WORLD WAR II

by Elizabeth Summers

Reading Consultant:
Barbara J. Fox
Professor Emerita
North Carolina State University

CAPSTONE PRESS
a capstone imprint

Blazers Books are published by Capstone Press,
1710 Roe Crest Drive, North Mankato, Minnesota 56003.
www.capstonepub.com

Library of Congress Cataloging-in-Publication Data

Summers, Elizabeth.
  Weapons and vehicles of World War II / by Elizabeth Summers.
      pages cm.—(Blazers books. Tools of war)
  Includes bibliographical references and index.
  Summary: "Describes various weapons and vehicles used by the Axis and Allied forces during
World War II"—Provided by publisher.
  Audience: Grades K-3.
  ISBN 978-1-4914-4080-3 (library binding)
  ISBN 978-1-4914-4114-5 (ebook pdf)
1. World War, 1939-1945—Equipment and supplies—Juvenile literature. 2. Vehicles, Military—
History—20th century—Juvenile literature. 3. World War, 1939-1945—Transportation—Juvenile
literature. I. Title.
  D743.7.S88 2016
  940.54—dc23   2015006162

Editorial Credits

Anna Butzer, editor; Heidi Thompson, designer; Jo Miller, media researcher;
Katy LaVigne, production specialist

Photo Credits

Alamy: INTERFOTO, 11(bottom), Photos 12, 21; Corbis: Don Trolani, 11(top); Getty Images: M.
McNeill, 14-15, Time & Life Pictures/George Silk; National Archives and Records Administration,
5, 7, 17, 22-23, 29; Newscom: akg-images, 25, KRT/US ARMY SIGNAL CORPS, 26, Sovfoto
Universal Images Group, 18-19; Shutterstock: Casper1774 Studio, 9 (top), zimand, 9 (bottom);
Wikimedia: U.S. Army Signal Corps, cover

Design Elements:
Shutterstock: angelinast, aodaodaodaod, artjazz, Brocreative, ilolab, kasha_malasha, Peter Sobolev

Printed in the United States of America in North Mankato, Minnesota.
052015   008823CGF15

TABLE OF CONTENTS

WAR OF THE WORLD

Two groups of nations fought during World War II (1939–1945). Germany, Italy, and Japan were the main Axis powers. The Axis planned to take over other countries. To stop the Axis nations, Great Britain, France, the United States, and other countries formed the Allies.

Fact

When World War II began, few could imagine the total ruin it would leave behind. More people died in World War II than in any other war.

Many kinds of weapons were used during World War II. Some of these weapons had been used before. Others were new or improved. A few weapons changed modern **warfare**.

Fact

Nuclear weapons were used for the first time during World War II.

warfare–the fighting of wars
nuclear weapon–the most dangerous kind of weapon in the world; the energy in nuclear weapons is created by splitting tiny particles of matter

WEAPONS

Pistols

Soldiers used pistols as **sidearms**. Two pistols became symbols of the different sides. German officers carried Lugers. U.S. troops carried Colt .45 semiautomatic pistols.

	Luger	Colt .45
Rate of Fire	semiautomatic	semiautomatic
Ammunition	9-mm bullets	.45 ACP cartridge
Weight	1.9 pounds (0.9 kg)	2.4 pounds (1 kg)

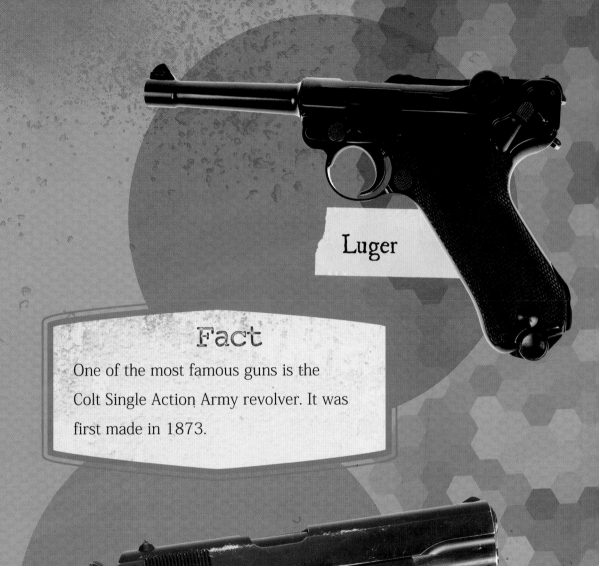

Luger

Fact

One of the most famous guns is the Colt Single Action Army revolver. It was first made in 1873.

Colt .45

sidearm–a weapon worn at the side or in the belt

Rifles

Soldiers also used rifles. Germans often carried Mauser rifles. Allied **snipers** hit targets from far away with the Mosin-Nagant.

	Mauser Karabiner 98K	Mosin-Nagant
Rate of Fire	15 rounds per minute	10 rounds per minute
Ammunition	7.92 x 57 mm bullets	7.62 x 54 mm bullets
Weight	8.2 pounds (3.7 kg)	8.8 pounds (4 kg)

sniper–a skilled military shooter who spots and hits targets from a hiding place
telescope–instrument made of lenses and mirrors that is used to view distant objects

Mauser Karabiner 98k

Fact

The Soviet Union made more than 300,000 Mosin-Nagant sniper rifles. Some of these sniper rifles had **telescopes**.

Mosin-Nagant

Both sides also used machine guns. Machine guns fire many bullets very quickly. The German MP40 submachine gun was designed for close **combat**.

	MP40 Submachine Gun	Browning Automatic Rifle	Sten Submachine Gun
Rate of Fire	500-550 rounds per minute	500-650 rounds per minute	500 rounds per minute
Ammunition	9 x 19 mm	7.62 x 63 mm	9 x 19 mm
Weight	8.7 pounds (3.9 kg)	15.8 pounds (7 kg)	7.1 pounds (3 kg)

combat–fighting between people or armies

Browning automatic rifle

Fact

Firing many bullets quickly makes machine gun barrels very hot. Some World War II machine guns used water to keep the barrels cool.

Explosives

Many explosive devices were used during the war. Soldiers carried hand **grenades**. **Mines** hidden underground or underwater blew up enemy targets.

grenade–a small bomb that can be thrown or launched
mine–an explosive device; water mines float in the water;
land mines are buried underground

	U.S. Pineapple Grenade	German Stick Grenade
Weight	1.3 pounds (0.6 kg)	1.3 pounds (0.6 kg)
How it Exploded	pullout pin to set off fuse	pull cord inside wooden handle to set off fuse
Time Before Explosion	4 seconds	4 seconds

Artillery

Both sides used powerful **artillery** weapons. These big guns destroyed land, sea, and air targets. The **howitzer** is an example of heavy artillery. Several people had to load, aim, and fire its heavy **shells**.

Fact

One large U.S. howitzer was nicknamed "Long Tom." It could hit targets up to 13 miles (21 kilometers) away.

artillery–large, powerful guns that are usually mounted on wheels or another supporting structure

howitzer–a cannon that shoots explosive shells long distances

shell–a hollow cartridge filled with an explosive that will explode on contact with a target

howitzer

VEHICLES

Tanks

Tanks had an important job during the war. They traveled over rough ground using tracks instead of wheels. Thick armor protected the soldiers inside.

	U.S. Sherman M4	Soviet T-34S	German Panzer IV Tiger
Weight	33.4 tons (30 mt)	29.2 tons (26 mt)	27.6 tons (25 mt)
Height	9 feet (2.7 m)	8 feet (2.4 m)	8 feet, 10 inches (2.6 m)
Speed	25-30 miles per hour (40-48 km/hr)	33 miles per hour (53 km/hr)	26 miles per hour (42 km/hr)
Number of Guns	3	3	3

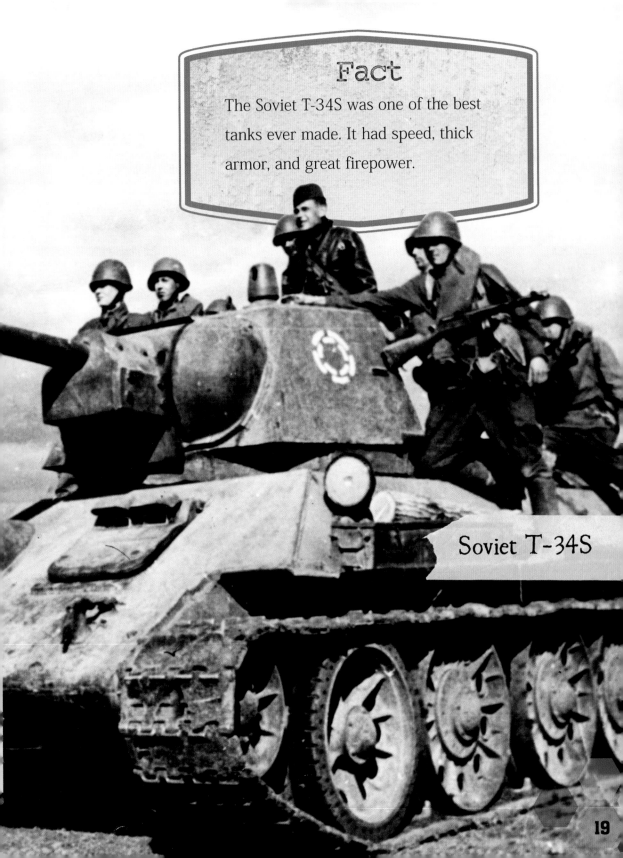

Soviet T-34S

Planes

Planes were one of the most important World War II vehicles. Bomber and fighter planes went on many dangerous missions over enemy land. Fighter planes are faster than bombers, but bombers carry heavier loads.

	U.S. B-24 Liberator Bomber	Japanese Zero Fighter Plane
Range	2,850 miles (4,587 km)	1,930 miles (3,106 km)
Speed	303 miles per hour (488 km/hr)	316 miles per hour (509 km/hr)
Weapons Carried	10 machine guns, 8,000 pounds of bombs	2 machine guns, 2 cannons, 2 66-pound bombs, 1 132-pound bomb

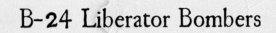

B-24 Liberator Bombers

range—the longest distance at which a weapon
can still hit its target

Ships

Ships also played a key role in the war. Ships carried soldiers and launched aircraft. They fired at land targets and fought other ships.

Aircraft carriers were the most important ships. The largest warships could each carry about 100 planes.

NEW TECHNOLOGIES

Several new weapons were used for the first time during World War II. Artillery weapons called bazookas launched shells that could destroy tanks. U.S. forces started using **flamethrowers** during World War II.

flamethrower—a weapon that shoots a stream of burning liquid

flamethrower

V-2 rocket

Germany invented amazing flying weapons. The Germans built the first long-distance rocket and the first fighter plane with a jet engine.

Fact

Germany's V-2 rocket was 46 feet (14 meters) long. It could fly at a speed up to 3,545 miles (5,705 km) per hour.

The United States made the first **atomic bomb**. Atomic bombs were dropped on two Japanese cities in 1945. Japan **surrendered** soon after the bombs exploded. World War II was over.

Fact

One atomic bomb has the explosive power of thousands of regular bombs.

atomic bomb—a bomb that produces an extremely powerful explosion when atoms are split apart
surrender—to give up or admit defeat

atomic bomb explosion

GLOSSARY

artillery (ar-TIL-uh-ree)—large, powerful guns that are usually mounted on wheels or another supporting structure

atomic bomb (uh-TOM-ik BOM)—a bomb that produces an extremely powerful explosion when atoms are split apart

combat (KOM-bat)—fighting between people or armies

flamethrower (FLAYM-throh-uhr)—a weapon that shoots a stream of burning liquid

grenade (gruh-NAYD)—a small bomb that can be thrown or launched

howitzer (HOU-uht-sur)—a cannon that shoots explosive shells long distances

mine (MINE)—an explosive device; water mines float in the water; land mines are buried underground

nuclear weapon (NOO-klee-ur WEP-uhn)—the most dangerous kind of weapon in the world; the energy in nuclear weapons is created by splitting tiny particles of matter

range (RAYNJ)—the longest distance at which a weapon can still it hits target

shell (SHEL)—a hollow cartridge filled with an explosive that will explode on contact with a target

sidearm (SIHD-ahrm)—a weapon worn at the side or in the belt

sniper (SNY-pur)—a skilled military shooter who spots and hits targets from a hiding place

surrender (suh-REN-dur)—to give up or admit defeat

telescope (TEL-uh-skohp)—instrument made of lenses and mirrors that is used to view distant objects

warfare (WAR-fayr)—the fighting of wars

READ MORE

Burgan, Michael. *Weapons, Gear, and Uniforms of World War II.* Equipped for Battle. Mankato Minn.: Capstone Pub., 2012.

Challen, Paul. *Mighty Tanks.* Vehicles on the Move. New York: Crabtree Publishing Company, 2011.

Fein, Eric. *Vehicles of World War II.* War Vehicles. North Mankato, MN: Capstone Pub., 2014.

INTERNET SITES

FactHound offers a safe, fun way to find Internet sites related to this book. All of the sites on FactHound have been researched by our staff

Here's all you do:

Visit *www.facthound.com*

Type in this code: 9781491440803

Check out projects, games and lots more at
www.CAPSTONEKIDS.com

INDEX